ESSENTIAL

SELLI

SUCCESSFULLY

D0106228

ROBERT HELLER

DK PUBLISHING, INC.

A DK PUBLISHING BOOK

www.dk.com

Produced for Dorling Kindersley
by Cooling Brown

Editor Jane Cooke
Designer Juliette Norsworthy
Creative Director Arthur Brown

DTP Designer Jason Little
Production Controller Silvia La Greca

Series Editor Adèle Hayward
Series Art Editor Tassy King
US Editors Gary Werner, Chuck Wills
Managing Editors Stephanie Jackson,
Jonathan Metcalf
Managing Art Editor Nigel Duffield

First American Edition, 1999
2 4 6 8 10 9 7 5 3

Published in the United States by
DK Publishing, Inc.
95 Madison Avenue, New York, New York 10016

Library of Congress Cataloging-in-Publication Data

Heller, Robert, 1932-
Selling successfully / by Robert Heller -- 1st American ed.
p.   cm. -- (Essential managers)
Includes index.
ISBN 0-7894-4864-5 (alk.paper)
1. Selling.   I. Title.   II. Series.
HD5438.25.H457 1999
658.85--dc21   99-15779
                                                CIP

Reproduced by Colourscan, Singapore
Printed in Hong Kong by Wing King Tong Co. Ltd.

CONTENTS

DEALING WITH CUSTOMERS

MAKING A
SUCCESSFUL SALE

MANAGING
SALES TEAMS

INTRODUCTION

Effective, high-performance selling is important to the success of almost every kind of business. Whether you are a salesperson working at the customer interface or a sales team manager, achieving the best possible results will be determined not only by your knowledge of your own product, but also by your understanding of your customers and the communication skills you can bring to bear to close a sale. Selling Successfully covers every aspect of the sales process, providing advice on taking the right mental approach, organizing yourself, understanding and working with your customers' needs, and building essential skills such as presenting and negotiating. It includes invaluable advice on running a sales team, and is supplemented by 101 useful tips scattered throughout the book. A self-assessment exercise helps you to evaluate and improve your skills.

PREPARING TO SELL

Selling is the basis of all business success. Lay the foundations for successful selling by following long-term principles and practices and by developing key personal skills.

AIMING FOR SUCCESS

In truly successful selling, everybody wins. Good salespeople make good deals for their customers. Bad salespeople give their customers bad deals. Customers who feel that they have made the right purchase will be happy and will be likely to come back for more.

MAKING A "WIN-WIN"

The win for salespeople is not just making the sale – the truly successful "win-win" consists of:
● Creating a satisfied customer;
● Earning satisfactory profits for the company.
The degree of satisfaction depends on the real strength of the proposition offered and delivered. Salespeople's performance tends to be judged on sales volume alone, which is simple to calculate, but can give a seriously misleading picture. This happens when, for example, the seller offers discounts or terms of trade that ultimately make that particular sale unprofitable.

Supportive sales manager recognizes the long-term benefits of the sale

PROMOTING CUSTOMER PARTNERSHIPS

The sales relationship most likely to result in a "win-win" is the supplier partnership. Many companies are giving all or much of their business to one or two suppliers and working closely with them. Any savings from the collaboration are often shared between the two parties. To form such a relationship with another party, you must invest time and effort in finding solutions to their needs. Be prepared to share business plans and to collaborate on research and development. Partnerships work best where power is balanced equally between the two parties. Where the purchaser dominates the relationship, take steps to strengthen your own position, and vice versa.

1 Find out what the customer really wants as early as possible.

Salesperson secures a deal that benefits his or her company's interests

↓

Customer realizes that the deal represents poor value for money

↓

Relationship between the salesperson and the customer ends

▲ MAKING A NO-WIN SALE
A salesperson who pursues a policy of making deals that are good for the seller but bad for the customer will ultimately fail to benefit from the value that a customer's long-term business represents.

◄ MAKING A WIN-WIN SALE
The ideal sale consists of a salesperson creating a satisfied customer, with the support of sales management, so that the business relationship continues.

Salesperson agrees to mutually beneficial terms

Customer receives the product or service that he wants

GAINING SELF-CONFIDENCE

Selling can sometimes seem like a form of confrontation. That explains why many salespeople find the process difficult or nerve-racking. Substitute positive expectations of success for negative fears of failure, and selling becomes an enjoyable experience.

2 Always approach prospective customers expecting to sell.

◀ **PACING YOUR SPEECH**
Speak clearly and succinctly, avoiding the temptation to rush.

PRESENTING CLEARLY

If you are nervous, you may be tempted to rush your sales pitch. Approach the sale with positive expectations, and deliver your lines at a steady pace. Speak with clarity and force, and avoid babbling. Look out for signs that your speech has delivered the message by watching the other party's body language, and by asking questions related to what you have just said. Always be prepared to slow down, and do not be afraid of silences.

ASSESSING YOUR SELF-CONFIDENCE

Answer "true" or "false" to these statements:
- My mind is my own.
- I can control my feelings.
- I can motivate myself.
- I do not need the approval of others.
- I follow my own principles of conduct.
- I do not complain if things go wrong.
- I have high self-esteem.
- I am not dependent on others.
- I do not blame and find fault.
- I do not worry about the future.
- I do not procrastinate.
- I do not get angry.
- I learn lessons from my failures.
- I treat others as I would expect to be treated myself.

Your answers should all be "true." If not, work on the areas concerned until all your answers are positive. This will provide a firm foundation for your self-confidence.

GIVING THE RIGHT IMPRESSION

How you look and behave has a direct bearing on confidence on both sides of the table. Dress with care, knowing that a well-pressed suit or outfit, like a neat haircut, conveys a message to the client. A good stance, direct eye contact, a firm handshake, and excellent manners all send positive messages. However, do not rely on your personal attributes and appearance to cover up inadequate preparation and knowledge. The effort to conceal ignorance and unreadiness creates insecurity, which will undermine your efforts to feel confident.

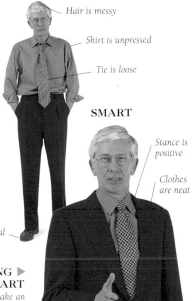

UNTIDY

Hair is messy

Shirt is unpressed

Tie is loose

SMART

Stance is positive

Clothes are neat

Shoes are casual

3 Take the advice of others about your appearance and your presence.

◀ **LOOKING THE PART**
Always make an effort to look well groomed and to appear positive.

COPING WITH REJECTION

The potential customer may not like you, what you are selling, or how you are selling it. The risk of being rejected by a customer is always daunting. The first lesson in building self-confidence is to understand that negative feelings are counterproductive and ill-founded. Be aware that what you think of yourself matters more than what you believe others think of you. Never say or think "no" for somebody else, but recognize that they, like you, have the right to refuse an offer. Remember that their refusal is not your failure, but their lost opportunity.

4 Have confidence in yourself if you want others to believe in you.

5 Record your presentation and correct any faults.

PRACTICING SELF-DEVELOPMENT

The best salespeople are ardent self-improvers. They read books, play tapes, videos, and CD-ROMs, and attend courses. These people know that paying attention to personal and professional development underpins successful careers.

6 Plan your reading and courses to meet specific, measurable aims.

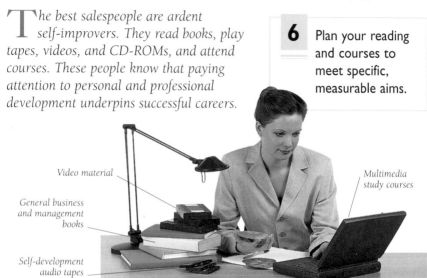

Video material

General business and management books

Self-development audio tapes

Multimedia study courses

WIDENING HORIZONS

Being a professional demands a comprehensive and up-to-date knowledge of the principles and practices of the profession. Widely available literature, CD-ROM and Internet courses, and videos on sales skills and techniques cover every sales activity. These "knowledge kits" are as important as specific product and company knowledge. General business and management books are important in giving background information, including accounts of how effective selling companies and salespeople have succeeded. They provide both factual information and inspirational impact.

▲ **KEEPING AHEAD**
Success is founded on knowledge gained from reading and study. Aim to know as much, if not more, than your customer to create an equal business relationship.

7 Revise your new knowledge at regular intervals, and keep practicing your acquired skills.

LEARNING FROM A MASTER

These ten maxims are derived from the *Golden Rules of Customer Care* written by top American car seller Carl Sewell:

- Ask customers what they want and give it to them again and again;
- Have systems that ensure you do the job right first time, every time;
- Under-promise, over-deliver;
- The answer to a customer is always "yes";
- Give every employee who deals with clients the authority to handle customer complaints;
- No complaints? Something is wrong;
- Measure everything;
- Pay people like partners;
- Show people respect;
- Learn best practice, imitate it, then improve it.

IMPROVING ABILITIES

All human activities can be improved by training, and most training can be self-taught. Every salesperson can markedly improve key critical personal abilities (see below). Gain as much knowledge of each ability as possible, and then aim to develop each one in turn. Make a personal development plan that includes a time-scale, a reading list, a schedule of courses, and, where relevant, targets for getting to the desired level of performance. When your objectives have been realized, set some new targets.

8 Try out selling maxims to see if they work for you.

9 Talk to others about what you learn. It will increase recall.

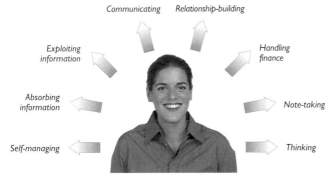

Communicating   Relationship-building

Exploiting information

Handling finance

Absorbing information

Note-taking

Self-managing

Thinking

◀ **TEACHING YOURSELF**
Improve your chances of selling successfully by learning how to use time more effectively (including how to speed-read and use short-hand). Develop skills for management accounting, handling conflict, and for increasing memory capacity and creativity.

GETTING ORGANIZED

Selling must be matched to very clear business purposes and planned to enable the realization of those aims. By organizing office documentation and systems, and by managing your time, your business aims will be met with greater ease and efficiency.

10 Track paperwork processes from start to finish to cut out waste.

CUTTING OUT PAPERWORK

Sales departments breed paper in large quantities. Aim to counteract this tendency as much as possible for two reasons: paperwork is demotivating to most salespeople; and much of it is unnecessary. Call reporting, in particular, can take up ten percent of a salesperson's time, without making any contribution to higher or better sales. Suggest reducing the number of forms used by your company to a minimum and making the forms as simple as possible. One approach is to abolish them all and then reintroduce only those that are missed. Remember that proper planning before selling is much more valuable than subjective accounts after a sales visit.

▲ **USING SUPPORT STAFF**
Delegate tasks such as filing to support staff when possible, leaving yourself free to concentrate on more productive activities.

11 Free an early morning period to catch up on undone tasks.

IMPROVING SYSTEMS

Use electronic documents whenever possible, rather than hard copies, to speed up reporting, to eliminate paper filing, and to make data easily transferable. Whether computerized or not, tailor forms to be built around the questions you want answered. You are only interested in accurate data and information that helps you to improve your performance and optimize business results.

USING TIME-LOGS

A time-log is a means of improving your use of time. Record your daily activities and note how much time you spend on them every day for two or three weeks. You may be surprised by how many tasks appear unnecessary or superfluous on reflection. List those activities that only you could have done, those that could have been delegated to subordinates, and those that did not need doing at all. If the latter have been ordered by superiors, take the matter up with those concerned. Your time is your most precious asset and it must not be squandered. Once the analysis is complete, replan your time around effective activities that you alone can do.

Period	Action
9.00–9.30	*Went through mail, faxes, and emails*
9.30–10.00	*Replied to all emails, including three personal ones*
10.00–10.30	*Introduced a new recruit to the rest of the sales team*
10.30–11.00	*Spoke to Norman about new computer equipment on order*
11.00–11.30	*Spoke to human resources about June's maternity leave entitlement*
11.30–12.00	*Made follow-up calls to five of our major customers*
12.00–12.30	*Chaired weekly sales meeting – continued through lunch hour*
12.30–1.00	*Sales meeting continued*
1.00–1.30	

▲ RECORDING ACTIVITIES
Divide your time-log into hourly or half-hourly slots, and record exactly how you spend your time each day. Use the log to pinpoint any wasted time.

12 Plan days daily, months monthly, and years annually.

CULTURAL DIFFERENCES

Attitudes to time vary from country to country. Germans dislike interruptions or changed schedules. The French work long hours because of long lunches. The British work longer hours than other Europeans, and Americans are the most likely to plan their working time strictly.

SETTING TARGETS

One super-salesman had a daily activity target of making four visits, writing four letters, and making four telephone calls. Similar discipline will pay off for anybody. Ask yourself what you want to accomplish each day, week, month, and year. Recording and revising these targets focuses your mind and enables you to ensure that enough time is available for each objective. If you find that each day is ending with targets unmet, reconsider how your time is spent. Almost certainly, nonessential activities are reducing the number of effective hours available to you.

USING ELECTRONIC AIDS

Selling and marketing have been moved into a new dimension with the advent of cyberspace. Portable computers and mobile telephones, to name just two modern devices, have become indispensable sales tools.

13 Contact people by telephone, fax, or email to avoid unnecessary visits.

EXPLOITING MOBILITY

Advances in telecommunications have created the salesperson of no fixed abode. One immediate advantage, apart from lower sales overheads, is the elimination of the need for coming into the office daily. Sales reporting can be handled over the computer network, automatically increasing the amount of selling time available. Face-to-face meetings, supplemented by conferencing – with or without video – remain essential, but can be planned only when necessary.

Mobile phone can be used to call clients from any location

MODERN SELLING ▶
The benefits of portable computers and telephones are considerable and enable salespeople to manage time effectively.

CARRYING COMPUTERS

Portable computers and electronic organizers have revolutionized key aspects of selling. The best equipped salespeople "carry" their desks and filing systems in their briefcases and have them linked to central office files. They can answer questions in customers' offices or homes at the click of a mouse. While talking to the customer, they can configure a potential order and check on availability, delivery, and prices. If a sale is made, they can enter the details immediately for clearing into the company system.

Portable allows salesperson to work at any temporary space

- The website should be viewed from the customer's point of view.
- What the customer needs to know should determine the content of your website.
- A trusted third party can make useful comments and criticisms on your site.
- All online inquiries should be answered within 24 hours.

OPERATING ONLINE

The Internet is potentially the greatest aid to selling ever invented. Every company can advertise using websites, and individual salespeople can set up their own sites. Some sites allow the customer to order, pay, and make queries without going near a salesperson. Companies of all sizes offer packages to help you get started on the Internet. You can have your website written, designed, programmed, and maintained, or you can choose to receive advice that enables your company to create and operate the site itself.

14 Make websites useful as well as useable.

◀ **SELLING BY EMAIL**
Unsolicited email can result in negative responses if it is seen as blanket mailing. Be selective when targeting potential customers for this form of marketing.

USING EMAIL AND FAX

Email, or electronic mail, has advantages in terms of cost and convenience compared with faxes. However, faxes are still heavily used – through both dedicated machines and computers. Email has the advantage of supplying an electronic version of the text, which the recipient can then manipulate, but faxes are more suitable for sending contracts and other legal documents requiring a signature. The prime advantage of email is also a main drawback – its ease of use results in a large number of messages. Encourage colleagues to send only important messages.

15 Act right away on any criticisms of your website.

16 Limit your email usage to business rather than personal matters.

DEALING WITH CUSTOMERS

Understanding customer attitudes is the key to increasing sales. Make an effort to research prospective customers, maximize customer contacts, and maintain strong relationships.

UNDERSTANDING TYPES OF CUSTOMER

The buying decisions of customers are influenced by many issues – not just competitive pricing, as is commonly supposed. Familiarize yourself with the range of customer needs, but keep an open mind when dealing with individuals.

17 Regard your customers as allies rather than as opponents.

18 Do research into customers' actual needs, and respond to findings.

DEVELOPING AWARENESS

Different customers have different needs over time, according to how their business is developing. While you should avoid pigeonholing customers, it is possible to recognize types and use this knowledge to target your products and techniques. Build up a profile of customers so you can emphasize features that are most attractive to them. Remember that by making people feel that your offering meets a basic need, they will feel justified in buying from you.

IDENTIFYING MOTIVES

Aim to match your sales strategy to your customer's motives and situation. Your customers will be receptive if you can offer a solution to their immediate problems or improve their business's performance. Some types of customer may be primarily motivated by security needs and will be looking for a guarantee of reliability. People who are driven by a desire to belong will buy what others buy, while those whose ego is the main motivator will want to be seen to have the best product available. Other customers, however, may be predisposed to reject your sales pitch without examining the potential benefits. In these cases, it is important not to waste time or lose heart.

19 Note that your customer's priorities probably differ from what you expect.

20 If you promise anything to your customer, always keep the promise.

RELATING TO THE CUSTOMER'S POSITION

POSITION	SIGNS	PROGNOSIS
GROWTH The customer perceives a gap between current and desired business performance.	Typically uses words like "more," "better," and "improve". This person is prepared to accept a proposal.	A good likelihood of sales success if you concentrate on showing that you can fill the perceived gap.
TROUBLE The customer is aware of a gap between required results and those that are achieved.	Will not admit to the difficulty directly, but may be prepared to discuss circumstantial problems.	The easiest type to sell to, if you can really fill the gap. Buyer is eager to say "yes" to somebody's proposal.
EVEN KEEL The buyer believes that the current position is satisfactory, and is unreceptive to change.	May use phrases such as "Don't rock the boat." Your proposal is seen as a threat, not an opportunity.	May switch to the Growth or Trouble position due to circumstances or persuasion – a hard sell otherwise.
OVERCONFIDENT This buyer thinks performance is satisfactory, rejects change, but may well be mistaken.	Will make it clear that "business has never been better," and that any change can only be for the worse.	Difficulties are almost certain to arise, but until they do, the chances of selling to this buyer are negligible.

FINDING CUSTOMERS

Making the right proposition to the right customer at the right time cannot be left to chance. Carry out research about customers and their companies before approaching them to increase the probability of finding the winning combination.

21 Pay equal attention to new and existing customers.

22 Save time and effort by targeting your sales drives.

IDENTIFYING PROSPECTS

New salespeople often think that the best sales prospects come from new customers. In fact, existing customers provide the best opportunities for sales, followed by former customers who have moved their business on. A common fault is to regard everyone as a potential customer, which can result in wasted effort. You want "qualified" prospects, or people who have been identified by market research as likely customers. These customers will have been identified by other companies, so competition may be strong.

FOLLOWING LEADS ▼
The pointers below indicate key sources of potential customers. Investigate each lead to establish a list of people who are most likely to buy your product or service. You can then focus your selling efforts on them.

Customers of the competition

People who have complained to the company

People who have made inquiries at the company

Those who have already been canvassed by your company

Personal acquaintances

Prospects identified by market research

Acquaintances of other staff

Respondents to direct mail

TARGETING THE BUYER

Salespeople can waste time by negotiating with someone who has no budget for a purchase, or who lacks the authority to say "yes" to the sales proposition. There is a tendency to make the sales approach at too low a level – because the salesperson feels uneasy dealing with senior people, or because he or she has not identified the key decisionmaker. Even if you know who the decisionmaker is, you may be unable to make direct contact. The key is to persevere. If you have identified a real need in a target company, the need will eventually outweigh the obstacles.

23 Spend time finding out who makes the final decision to buy in the target company.

▼ **MAKING CONTACT**
Find out who has the ultimate buying power, and persist in making contact. Existing and former customers are especially worth pursuing at senior levels as they yield the best results.

CONTACTING CUSTOMERS

Establish a well-researched list of prospective customers

⬇

Double-check the name and title of the person you need to deal with

⬇

Initiate contact with prospective customers by telephone, letter, or both

⬇

Confirm proposals and meeting times by letter

RESEARCHING CUSTOMERS

Y ou can discover much about potential
customers without leaving your desk.
Once you have identified a prospective
client, spend time learning about his or
her needs and aspirations while constantly
looking for opportunities to increase sales.

24 Work closely with
customers to find
the best selling
opportunities.

CARRYING OUT RESEARCH

Y our desk is where to begin asking some vital
questions about potential customers. Use these
as starting points. Against the questions, write
where the information can be found – in your
own files, on relevant websites, or through
personal contacts – to make your research more
time efficient. Next, brief yourself thoroughly on
your own company and its offer, and on the
competition – your own and the customer's.

◀ FINDING KILLER OPPORTUNITIES
*Research your client's needs and
desires to discover "killer
opportunities" that customers will
clamor for. Aim to sell a product
or service that delivers so much
competitive advantage the
opposition cannot compete.
Such products or services are
known as "killer applications."
The term comes from the field of
Information Technology and was
originally applied to software
applications that were so popular,
people bought new computers just
to run them on. To interest the
customer in finding such a
winning product or service,
research and present examples
from other businesses.*

IDENTIFYING NEEDS

Thorough knowledge of the customer's business and requirements is fundamental. It will help you to pinpoint the factors most likely to close a deal. Emphasize the following outcomes if they are likely to meet the needs of the prospective customer:

- Improved performance and better results;
- A product or service that is new to the buyer and will offer valuable benefits;
- Greater value for money;
- An opportunity to strengthen the buyer's position in the company;
- Removing a serious problem or bottleneck;
- Rivaling or outreaching the competition.

25 Find out about customers from the best source – your customers.

26 Think about the customer as your most valuable business asset.

27 Concentrate on the benefits that your company will be able to supply.

EXPANDING SALES

While researching your customers, endeavor to discover the wider business needs that promise further and larger sales. The sale of a product system complete with components, for example, is much more valuable than selling a component alone. By looking beyond the immediate product and its characteristics, you can expand the size of your selling proposition.

DO YOU KNOW YOUR CUSTOMER?

It is easy to concentrate on product knowledge, but much harder to gain a thorough understanding of the customer. Use the following statements as a checklist. Make sure you adapt your strategy and tactics according to any insight gained.

I have learned everything I need to know about my customer and the product I am selling.

I know what the customer really wants and what I really want to sell.

I have checked who makes or influences the buying decision and which influences are sympathetic.

I understand the customer's current and potential business worth in profit terms.

COMMUNICATING EFFECTIVELY

Your key objective when communicating with a customer is to secure a sale. Ideally, a meeting should result in a satisfactory outcome for both parties. Honest and open communication is the key.

28 Adapt your style to that of your customer.

BEING OPEN

You must be confident in order for your customer to have confidence in you. Eye contact and body language play a very important part in building rapport. Smile and use open, nonthreatening gestures. Watch the customer's body language for clues as to how they are responding to you, and modify your behavior accordingly. Question and listen instead of making statements, and take careful note of objections and complaints – they may give you further clues as to the needs of the customer.

29 Do not be afraid of silences – use them to collect your thoughts.

Open arms indicate customer is receptive to suggestions

Body language remains positive throughout meeting

◄ KEEPING POSITIVE
Be positive and honest when communicating. Lean forward, make eye contact, and emphasize key points with hand gestures.

USING COMMUNICATION TECHNIQUES

TECHNIQUES	KEYS TO ACHIEVEMENT
EMPATHY Put yourself in the customer's shoes to help you understand the issues from his or her point of view.	● Ask for as much information as possible about the other person in a genuine, straightforward manner. ● Use questions that encourage openness. ● Be supportive in your pose, nodding or making approving noises to show that you are listening.
RESEARCH Find out about the facts surrounding a customer's situation to understand why they think as they do.	● Ask the customer open questions to draw out as much information as possible. ● Keep the emphasis on fact-finding. ● Listen to the answers carefully for clues that will help you understand more about the other person.
SYNTHESIS Aim to resolve any conflicts and guide the discussion towards a desired objective.	● Make statements that will encourage the other party to respond constructively. ● Show by your responses that you value what they have said and that their responses have influenced your actions.
NEUROLINGUISTIC PROGRAMMING (NLP) Use this technique to attain conversational harmony with the customer.	● While listening intently, match your spoken language and body language to that of the customer. ● Mirror the customer's imagery, phraseology, posture, and gestures, modifying any that are counterproductive.
BODY LANGUAGE Use positive body language to encourage the customer to move toward a commitment or to adopt your ideas.	● Keep an open posture – relax your arms, lean forward, slightly tilt the head, and avoid slouching. Maintain eye contact and keep smiling. ● Respond with reassuring gestures if the customer betrays signs of nervousness or negativity.
CLEAR REACTIONS Show that you have listened to and understood the other person by responding directly to their concerns and requests.	● Listen for any concerns that may be underlying a discussion and seek to resolve them. ● Follow up requests promptly; if you cannot deliver the full promise at once, explain why and say when the promise will be kept.

MOTIVATING CUSTOMERS

Getting a prospective customer on your side means striving to recognize what motivates him or her. That will seem easier when the customer is friendly and informative. If the customer initially shows hostility, work hard to overcome the barrier between you. There are two key behaviors that motivate customers. The first is empathy: put yourself in the other person's position, talk straightforwardly, and use gentle persuasion when the customer seems uncertain. Get to the point quickly if someone is busy or impatient. The second is projection: use your strength of character to gain compliance. The best way to motivate a customer is to use a combination of the two techniques.

30 Complete all the research you can before meeting the customer.

▼ **ASKING FOR FEEDBACK**
If a customer appears hostile or confused, encourage him or her to provide you with feedback, however negative, in the hope that you can allay any fears.

Salesperson solicits feedback in an open and friendly manner

CULTURAL DIFFERENCES

When communicating internationally, cultural factors must be considered. Japanese customers, for example, can be hard for others to read. They may say little during a meeting, yet suddenly make an offer. You may have to wait before the French get to the point of a long business lunch. The British like a give-and-take conversation, which may even end inconclusively. Americans may show great enthusiasm for your offer, but may not accept it.

ANSWERING QUESTIONS

How do you handle questions when you do not know the answers? If possible, do not admit your ignorance, since it undermines your credibility. One technique is to answer a question with another question. When asked "Who is your biggest competitor?", for instance, reply "Do you think that size is the crucial factor in your market?". At some point, however, you must be able to show knowledge of the market. Always listen carefully to questions before answering them, and use positive body language to reinforce your answers.

31 Avoid speculating about how a meeting went.

32 Encourage customers to reveal their aims.

33 Always strive to obtain feedback from the customer toward the end of a meeting.

Customer's body language shows hostility to proposition

STEERING DISCUSSIONS

Customers will influence the course of the discussion, and may be working to their own agenda. They may seem unwilling to listen to you or to discuss issues that you want to cover. Keep returning to your strategy after handling queries with sympathy and honesty:
● Do not be led easily into repetitive debate;
● Counter arguments toward the end of a meeting in which you have successfully put across your main points;
● Respond to all of the customer's arguments with total honesty.

PROVIDING CUSTOMER SERVICE

Treat sales and customer service as one and the same. Regard sales as a front-line activity – looking after customers' needs by providing what they want, when, and how they want it, and by following up the sale to ensure they are satisfied.

34 Check up on the effectiveness of your service by personal trial.

35 Monitor customer response, and act immediately if you find it inadequate.

36 If customers complain, assume they are right.

RESPONDING TO CUSTOMER INQUIRIES

An essential aspect of sales is responding to customer inquiries, but it is often badly handled. Figures for responses on the World Wide Web highlight the problem. Only two out of ten contactors get replies within a day, and 13 percent of people receive no response at all. Ideally all inquirers should get a response the same day. Always answer your telephone – it is counterproductive to avoid contact with customers.

RESPONSES TO ▶ WEB INQUIRIES
World Wide Web sites have been set up on the Internet to generate sales inquiries and, presumably, to answer them. Yet most companies are failing to take advantage of this fast-growing sales medium, as the figures on this chart show.

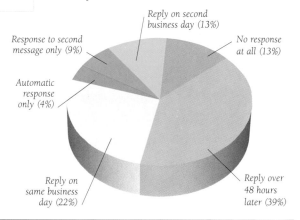

Reply on second business day (13%)

No response at all (13%)

Response to second message only (9%)

Automatic response only (4%)

Reply on same business day (22%)

Reply over 48 hours later (39%)

DEALING WITH COMPLAINTS

All customers who complain are valuable assets. The complaints tell you necessary truths about the quality of your company's product or service. By handling complaints swiftly and effectively, you create a high degree of customer satisfaction:

● Apologize and own the problem;
● Act quickly – within five days;
● Assure the customer the problem is being fixed;
● Deal with it in person or on the telephone.

You must make it clear at the outset that you are 100 percent on the customer's side. Even if the complaint is factually unjustified, the client's perception is otherwise and that perception is what matters. Never rest until the matter has reached a conclusion acceptable to the customer.

CUSTOMER CONFIDENCE

When handling complaints, follow these rules to retain customer confidence and avoid antagonizing them further:

● Paraphrase the customer's complaint to show that you have heard and understood.
● Tell the customer that you understand how they feel.
● Assure the customer that their feedback is invaluable.
● Apologize for any inconvenience, and do all you can to make up for it.

37 Establish a habit of calling your customers after a sale to check that they are satisfied.

▼ MONITORING PROGRESS
Endeavor to maintain client contact and continue to reinforce customer relationships whatever the size of the sale.

MAINTAINING CONTACT

Customer service must not end with the sale. How well you identify with and handle the needs of the customers has a marked effect on their loyalty. The principle is the same with a machinery buyer or a vacation customer: always ask "Is the customer satisfied?" and "Will he or she buy again?". If the answers are "No," find out why and what can be done about it. Make a note to call customers regularly to check levels of satisfaction.

Call your customers regularly to check they are satisfied

Make a note of any complaints and act on them immediately

SATISFYING CUSTOMERS

You can never satisfy all of the customers all of the time. But you can never stop trying to do so. Find out what the customer's requirements are, and then discover whether those needs have been met by constantly monitoring the customer's reactions.

38 Keep first-class service standards to please and retain customers.

ESTABLISHING PRIORITIES

The primary target of selling – to exceed customer expectations and earn an "excellent" rating from clients – depends on knowing in advance what matters most to the buyer. Do not assume that price is the top priority. Salespeople often damage profits by taking this for granted. Customers may have a number of different factors on their list of priorities, such as delivery times or technical support. If you have researched what customers want most, and how your company's product or service ranks against the competition, then successful selling will be considerably easier.

Read company reports to assess the needs of your customers

▲ **RESEARCHING NEEDS**
Use all sources available to research your customers, from company literature to press reports.

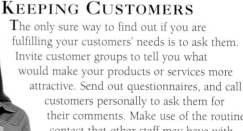

ASSESSING ▶ PRIORITIES
Keep an open mind about what your customer values the most about your propositions.

Use customer feedback to establish their priorities

KEEPING CUSTOMERS

The only sure way to find out if you are fulfilling your customers' needs is to ask them. Invite customer groups to tell you what would make your products or services more attractive. Send out questionnaires, and call customers personally to ask them for their comments. Make use of the routine contact that other staff may have with customers, since they may be able to provide useful insights. Above all, make it clear to customers that you want their comments and will act on them.

MEETING CUSTOMER NEEDS

QUESTIONS TO ASK	ACTIONS TO TAKE
BRAND AND IMAGE Does your company and its products have a strong rating in the marketplace?	● Find out if the customer has a high opinion of the brand and the company. ● Check if the customer feels that they are buying the right product from the right company.
SALES TECHNIQUE Is the sales process being conducted so that the customer likes doing business with your company?	● Provide your salespeople with training in customer care and communication skills. ● Establish that the buyer is being helped to make the right decision and is not being put under pressure.
KEEPING COMMITMENTS Is your company doing what it says it will, when it says it will?	● Deliver the right product to the right place at the right time in the right quantity. ● Live up to your word, and avoid making promises that you may not be able to fulfill.
ADMINISTRATION Is the sale being handled with efficiency and without unnecessary bureaucratic procedures?	● Ensure that invoices and other documents are clear and accurate and easy to use correctly. ● Encourage your company to be flexible in drawing up and interpreting terms and conditions.
RESPONSIVENESS Is the customer being answered and responded to swiftly and effectively at all times?	● Clarify any ambiguous communications with the customer as soon as possible. ● Deal with customer's complaints by acknowledging mistakes and rectifying errors immediately.
INFORMATION Does the customer know everything that they need to know about the product or service they are buying?	● Make sure that your salespeople are knowledgeable about the product or service they are supplying. ● Provide the customer with all the information and assistance needed to use the product or service.
PRODUCT OR SERVICE Does the purchase live up to or exceed the customers expectations?	● Ensure that agreed specifications are met, including any special concessions made when negotiating the sale. ● Check that the customer is happy with the performance of the service or product.
AFTER-SALES SERVICE Is the customer relationship being looked after successfully post-sale?	● Make sure that customer inquiries or complaints are always dealt with promptly and courteously. ● Be proactive in contacting the customer to monitor how satisfied they feel with their purchase.

39 Employ proven research firms to measure customer satisfaction.

40 Back up survey results by posing questions to a customer sample.

MEASURING SATISFACTION

Customer satisfaction must be researched, and preferably measured. There are two main types of research method: quantitative and qualitative. Quantitative research, usually based on questionnaires, can be measured for statistical analysis. "Closed" questions are used, which means responses are limited – for example, to a scale of one to five. This type of research is very well-established and widespread, but fairly expensive. You should supplement quantitative results with qualitative research, which is based on interviews. Both methods should be carried out as part of your follow-up routine to ensure that the customer remains content.

QUANTITATIVE SURVEYS

This type of survey uses questions that prompt specific answers from customers, since the results are calculated for use in charts and tables. But do not assume that all such results are accurate. Errors can be introduced, and a high score may conceal customer dissatisfaction that will have a serious impact on future sales. Research by Xerox has shown that customers who give a "Very Satisfied" rating, for instance, are six times more likely to buy from you again than those registering as "Satisfied." So, if the questions used in quantitative surveys are not clearly defined (if "Very Satisfied" and "Satisfied" are combined, for example), results can be misleading.

Ask if customers would buy from you again

Ask if customers would be prepared to recommend you to other people

Ask if customers would rate your product or service as excellent

Assess the customers' response, and make any changes that are necessary

POSING KEY QUESTIONS ▶
Quantitative research, like an opinion poll, poses identical questions to a representative sample of people. Any research should address three basic questions that really matter when assessing customer satisfaction. If your research provides you with customer responses to each of these questions, you will have your essential research information.

▼ USING TEST PANELS AND FOCUS GROUPS

An external researcher may ask questions of panels, or focus groups, if the company has many customers (such as a retail chain). This research is most effective when carried out in an informal setting.

QUALITATIVE SURVEYS

The qualitative survey method involves asking customers personally how they feel about a product or service. The survey uses questions that encourage customers to volunteer their feelings. It can be conducted in-house or out-of-house. In-house methods often involve either group interviews with a customer panel or individual interviews as follow-ups to questionnaires. Face-to-face, in-depth interviews are the most telling methods, but you should take care not to influence the answers. Ask "What do you think of the service?", rather than "Do you think the service is good?".

COMMUNICATING SENSIBLY

Just as you can over-sell to the customer, so you can overdo the effort to delight. Companies are now encouraged to embark on "relationship marketing," which provides (and often bombards) the customer with follow-up letters, telephone calls, and special offers. Keep follow-up activities within careful control. Have a clear reason for each act of communication, and do not make too frequent calls on the customer's time and patience. On the other hand, never fail to accept or return a customer's call or to reply promptly to any correspondence. Failure to do so can undo much hard-won customer loyalty.

41 Good is not good enough – only excellence takes you forward.

42 Pose as a customer to test how your company handles customer calls.

MAKING A SUCCESSFUL SALE

Effective selling involves planning and strategy. Your strategy may initially involve a team presentation or a simple mail shot, but all sales ultimately depend on negotiating skills.

PLANNING THE APPROACH

Selling operations need military-style planning to improve success rates. The customers must be clearly identified, the market properly covered – with salespeople covering carefully allocated areas – and the sale must match customer needs.

43 Make sure your sales strategy makes sense to everybody.

44 Assess your brand image and current market position to strengthen your sales strategy.

ADOPTING A STRATEGY

Whether you are selling an existing product, or launching a new one, a successful sales strategy is based on a thorough analysis of product, market, and competition. Your strategy may be aimed at finding new customers, or at building strong relationships with existing customers. But before you commit resources to a sales drive, consider the size of the market, its potential, and the strength of competition from other organizations. Once you have established your market, ensure that your sales force covers the areas in which customers or potential customers are located.

45 Look for the most exciting customer propositions.

FOLLOWING A SALES STRATEGY

> **Investigate the customer's objectives by desk research and by asking colleagues**

> **Plan an arresting presentation, keeping the cutomer's objectives in mind**

> **Make your presentation, supplying as much information as possible**

> **Negotiate terms that meet both your goals and the needs of the customer**

> **Close the deal, summarizing the key points and emphasizing benefits**

SELLING IN STAGES

Your selling process should go through key stages before you attempt to close a deal. Each of these stages requires its own mini-plan. Set down your desired outcome, the tactics you will employ to win that outcome, and your response to foreseeable deviations. Revise your plan at every stage to incorporate any new knowledge or information you have gleaned. Your assessment of the customer's needs and expectations will provide the starting point for planning your sales and negotiation strategies and your presentation. Ensure that you have all the relevant facts and figures available to enable you to answer any questions the customer may have, and always conclude a meeting by reiterating the unique benefits of your product or service.

KNOWING YOUR PRODUCT AND MARKET

A successful sales strategy depends on the key skills of persuasion and negotiation – skills that can only be effectively deployed if they are reinforced by familiarity with, and confidence in, the product or service being offered. Customers rely on salespeople to tell them what they need to know, so it is essential that you have the answers for any line of enquiry that might arise. It is not sufficient to limit your knowledge to your own product – you must be able to put it into context with similar products so that favorable comparisons can be made. Use every method available to become an expert in your field. Study market literature, discuss relevant issues with technical, operations, and production staff, and take advantage of training. Above all, use every sales call as an opportunity to increase your knowledge, and therefore your competence.

USING AIDCA

The acronym AIDCA stands for the key words Attention, Interest, Desire, Conviction, and Action. These are the five stages that you should lead your prospective customer through in sequence to maximize the chances of a successful sale.

FOLLOWING AIDCA PRINCIPLES

Direct-mail sellers have long used the AIDCA formula as a guide to writing sales letters. But the principles apply strongly to all aspects of selling. Following them gives you an organizing tool that provides your sales pitch with shape and direction, and makes the proposition coherent as well as attractive to the prospective customer. First catch the customer's Attention, then arouse Interest. Convert Interest into Desire for your product or service before creating the Conviction that will result in Action – the sale.

ATTRACTING ATTENTION

You neet to gain the attention of the customer in order to make a sale. Attention can be grabbed by an all-singing, all-dancing act, by an arresting proposition, or by an introduction from an influential or admired person. Whatever technique you use, your aim is to be noticed. Assume that the customer is besieged with propositions and proposers. Carefully design your opening gambit, whether delivered in person, over the telephone, or in writing, to distinguish yourself from the competition. You have to win the customers' eyes and ears before you can win their minds, hearts, and wallets.

46 Work hard on developing a "story" that will interest buyers.

47 Consider how to grab attention in a mail shot.

ATTENTION

Salesperson writes an arresting mail shot

▲ **AIDCA IN ACTION**
The first stages in the sequence determine whether your approach will be successful. Make your mail shot as striking as possible, and include interesting information that will tempt the reader to find out more.

48 Keep "features" in reserve as aids to tip the balance to your advantage.

49 Make the best possible use of the first minutes with the customer.

DEVELOPING INTEREST

Capitalize on Attention by turning it into Interest. This depends on understanding and pressing a customer's "hot-spot." That is the promise (explicit or implicit) that the potential purchase will meet a genuine customer need. "What I have to offer will halve your telephone bills" is the kind of proposition that is likely to interest anybody. On its own, the statement that excites Interest will not make a sale. It sets up the customer to be receptive to further information.

Key points in the mail shot arouse customer interest

INTEREST

DESIRE

Salesperson meets customer to provide extra information and stimulate desire

INSPIRING DESIRE

Attention and Interest are not enough to clinch a sale. The customer has to be brought to a condition of Desire. The process of booking a vacation illustrates the progression. An advertisement in the press attracts Attention, the details about the resort arouse Interest, and the pictures in the brochure sent by a travel agent inspire Desire. The extras, like discounts or preferential payment schemes, provide additional attraction. The basic need is all-important, but the embellishments can tip the scale and, in some cases, can be seen as the main objects of Desire.

50 Ask yourself "Why is my product unique?" and use the answer.

Customer realizes offer is unbeatable

CONVICTION

INCITING ACTION

The test of effectiveness is Action. The famous sales pitch "Act now while supplies last" sums up two key principles: immediacy and urgency. You want the customer to place their order now, so you make it appear that the opportunity will not last for ever. This situation may be artificial, but unless elements of urgency can be created, the sales process may drag on, and impetus may be lost. Then the whole AIDCA sequence will have to be repeated, with lower chances of success. Properly timed, the sequence is logical and highly effective.

CREATING CONVICTION

The customer must be drawn to the conclusion that they must buy from you, and you alone. In advertising terms, you must present the Unique Selling Proposition, or USP. This is the attribute that persuades the buyer that your product or service is different and better. Comparing a vacation with more expensive alternatives, for example, encourages the Conviction that the buying decision is correct. So does an attractive insurance package, or a concession on payment methods. The more you let customers convince themselves, as opposed to being convinced, the better for the sale.

◀ CONCLUDING THE SALE
The final stages in the AICDA sequence aim to persuade the customer that they will not get a better deal elsewhere, and to make the decision to buy.

ACTION

Salesperson urges customer to act promptly to avoid missing out

Customer decides to purchase

51 Give customers a final incentive to "sign on the dotted line."

52 Employ jokes and vivid words to engage clients.

CHANGING PREFERENCES

The object of AIDCA is to persuade the buyer to prefer your offering to all alternatives and, you hope, to shift from their current product or service to yours. The most effective method is to offer the best solution to the buyer's identified problems, and to demonstrate the solution when possible. Putting yourself across as a humorous and helpful person who is strongly associated with the company or brand assists the sale. Provide vivid descriptions of the beneficial results of buying from you, and give the customer plenty of news about new features and applications. Novelty needs backing with security, so come armed with testimonials from satisfied clients.

Customer tries out the product first-hand

Salesperson demonstrates product benefits

◀ **DEMONSTRATING A PRODUCT**
Do not forget the power of demonstrations, if applicable, to create the Conviction that will eventually result in Action.

DO'S AND DON'TS

✔ Do stress the unique benefits that can be obtained by buying from you.

✔ Do focus on the last "A" in AIDCA: get the customer to act now.

✘ Don't "knock" rivals when convincing clients that they should buy from you.

✘ Don't let the sales process drag on if AIDCA has failed.

53 Use "free" or extra features to help persuade the customer to buy.

COMMUNICATING BY MAIL

Writing is required for most types of selling, so the better its quality, the higher the likely volume of sales. Direct mail, which relies upon excellent writing, is a highly effective and fast-growing sales method – a whole selling campaign can be based on it.

54 Have your letters read by someone else to help spot any errors.

55 Test different letters on groups of customers and select the best.

56 Make sure that all mailed material reinforces your brand values.

WRITING FOR SUCCESS

Letters are effective sales methods to use as introductions and as precursors to direct mail shots. If you receive a letter in response, never allow it to go unanswered, and always follow it up by telephone. If your correspondence is successful and you meet the customer, write to confirm what has been discussed (a letter then acts like the minutes of the meeting), and to advance the negotiation. Always ensure that matters of substance are recorded on paper. Finally, if the sale should fall through, do not forget to send a letter that is designed to keep you in mind for future opportunities.

IMPROVING YOUR WRITING

Use the following guidelines, which follow the principles of AIDCA, to write an excellent introductory letter that will grab and hold the customer's attention.

- Plan ahead, giving your writing an introduction, middle, and short end.
- Improve your physical writing speed.
- Write as you talk – naturally.
- Visualize the reader and address them.
- Use as few words as you need.

- Make sure that your meaning is clear.
- Keep your sentences simple and short.
- Preserve a smooth and logical flow.
- Never strive for effect.
- Avoid circumlocutions and archaisms.
- Use short words rather than long ones.
- Use active voice instead of passive voice.
- Avoid jargon and double negatives.
- Speak your written words to yourself.
- Revise only when you have finished.

SELLING BY MAIL

Direct-mail selling eliminates telephone calls. It also allows for controlled experiments – varying sales methods until you find a combination that attracts the most custom. Writing an effective letter is obviously vital, but the most important factor is the mailing list. It is essential to have an up-to-date list of potential customers, either compiled from your own database, or bought in from a mailing-list company. Sending out large mailings is expensive, and the letter should always be tested first on a small, random sample to ensure that profit on the investment will more than cover the costs of preparation, printing, and postage.

Logo adds corporate identity

◀ **ELEGANT DESIGN**
Spend time choosing the style of your direct mail shots. The design should be clear, consistent, and eye-catching

Consistent style reinforces brand recognition

RECOGNIZING BRANDS

Organizations spend heavily on brochures and other material, which is distributed by mail, at trade fairs, or on sales visits. The materials vary from glossy leaflets to price lists. Whatever its nature and cost, any production must answer one key question: "Will it give the customer clear reasons to buy from us, and nobody else?". That means adopting a consistent, high-quality design to sustain brand recognition, delivering messages with clarity and impact, and avoiding an excessive and dense quantity of material.

WRITING AN EFFECTIVE DIRECT MAIL LETTER

Promise the most important product benefit at the very beginning

Enlarge upon the benefit (or benefits) immediately after the opening

Tell the reader what they are going to get in as much detail as possible

Back up the product or service details with proof of sales and endorsements

Tell the reader what they may lose if they fail to take up the offer

Rephrase the prominent benefits in the closing section of your mail shot

Incite action – let the reader know that they must act immediately

USING THE TELEPHONE

*P*ersuading a customer by telephone to
meet you, especially someone who has
never heard of you, is a sales skill in itself.
Use well-practiced telephone techniques
for establishing contact, booking meetings,
and selling direct by telephone.

> **57** Arrange to meet
> your customer face
> to face, however
> hard it may seem.

BREAKING THE ICE

It is important to give a valid reason for your call.
Try developing an initial icebreaker for securing
appointments over the telephone. Suitable questions
are: "Has anybody visited you from Selling Inc.,
lately?"; or "Has my name been mentioned?". Your
answer, whatever the reply, needs to be positive.
"Did you get my letter?" can be used if you have
made initial contact by letter. Make a point of
following up any correspondence with a telephone
call. If the other party cannot remember your
letter or its contents, you have the perfect
opportunity to explain your reason for calling.

POINTS TO REMEMBER

- Matching your vocal pace to that
  of the person you are talking to
  will establish a rapport.
- Interrupting the other party
  should be avoided.
- The use of "I" should be kept to
  a minimum; instead use your own
  name five times during the call.
- On the first call, "This is" rather
  than "My name is" makes a good
  opening.
- Pauses should be avoided during
  your telephone conversation.

*Hold the
telephone firmly*

*Have a script in
front of you*

*Look at a mirror
to encourage you
to smile*

◀ **IMPROVING
TECHNIQUES**
*Securing an appointment by
telephone will be assisted by
concentrated effort. Preparing a
script and monitoring your facial
expressions in a mirror will help
you achieve a positive outcome.*

Maintaining Interest

When dealing with a customer, show genuine interest in them. Ask, "How are you?" as if the automatic answer ("Fine, thanks") is meaningful. If either party has limited the call, say, to ten minutes, do not exceed this limit unless the other party plainly wants to carry on. Ensure that you maintain a sympathetic response, even if the conversation becomes objectionable and includes criticisms. Use stock responses like "That's understandable," or "We find that is the case with most people."

58 Like the people you deal with, and show your liking in word and deed.

59 Confirm the time before you leave for a meeting.

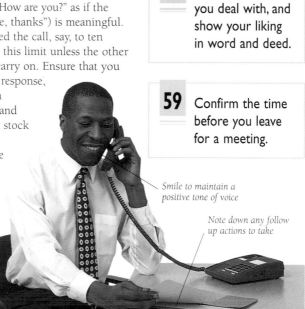

Smile to maintain a positive tone of voice

Note down any follow up actions to take

◀ REMAINING POSITIVE
Make the customer feel that you are on his or her side. React to any hostility with sympathy, and always keep calm. Avoid making promises you cannot fulfil.

Securing an Appointment

When cold-calling strangers to get an appointment, you should expect to succeed every time. Explain briefly the reason for the call, and use these questions or statements to help secure a meeting, which you must confirm before ringing off:

❝ *You've probably heard my name already. Has anybody mentioned me to you?* ❞

❝ *As you may know, Selling Inc. has recently introduced the first fully digital* ❞

❝ *I'd be happy to drop by and give you the opportunity to learn about this new product.* ❞

❝ *I'll be in your area on Tuesday around 3 p.m. Will you be there for seven minutes if I drop by?* ❞

MAKING THE MOST OF MEETINGS

O nce you have made the effort to understand your customers' needs and objectives, you can start to plan how to use your time with them effectively, and how to present your sales proposition so that it is as attractive as possible.

60 Only give your customers product information that they really want.

PLANNING CUSTOMER MEETINGS

Every aspect of a customer contact needs to be carefully thought out. Choose a neutral location, and remember that formality helps concentration, but may be intimidating. Conversely, a relaxed environment can be unbusinesslike. Be clear about your objective – is it to make a sale or to build up data on customer needs? Ensure that you have all the facts and figures on your own and rival products. Estimate the time it will take to cover the essential points, and have copies of relevant data – a brochure, for example – that you can leave with the customer. Always be clear about how much you are prepared to compromise.

PROMOTING YOUR PRODUCT

When you meet the customer, ensure that you provide all the information that they need to choose your product or service:

● Tell the customer what you know of his or her current activities and ambitions;

● Stress how your product can benefit the customer;

● Elaborate on product or service features, benefits, and company knowledge;

● Know your competitors' strengths and weaknesses, and be knowledgeable about their products and services:

● Anticipate negative points that the customer may raise, and be ready with positive remedial suggestions;

● Provide references from satisfied customers.

DO'S AND DON'TS

✔ Do plan questions that will get a positive response.

✔ Do allow time to listen to the customer.

✔ Do memorize all the unique aspects of your offer and the company.

✘ Don't overwhelm the customer by including too much information.

✘ Don't plan to bully the buyer into the deal.

✘ Don't worry about failure – expect to be successful.

LISTENING TO CUSTOMERS

Allow customers to tell you what they need before you tell them what you have to offer, and ask questions to ensure that you have understood them. Always be courteous, addressing the customer by name, and avoid jargon. Aim to exceed expectations by asking the customer if there is anything that might make your product or service more attractive. Try to end a meeting by offering them an extra, unsolicited concession (however small) to make them feel that they are a favoured customer. Thank them for their time, and tell them how much you value their custom.

61 Be aware of your objective when planning a customer meeting.

CULTURAL DIFFERENCES

American salespeople are known for giving slick presentations when meeting customers. The British are often shy about selling and will take time getting to the point of the meeting. Germans are more formal and may use meetings mainly to give the customer a mass of product information. A French salesperson may take an intellectual approach and do most of the talking.

62 Be absolutely sure that your company is able to deliver any service promises that you make.

MAKING ▼ FOLLOW-UP CALLS
It is usually appropriate to follow up meetings with a telephone call. This will establish a relationship with the customer and keep you uppermost in their minds.

Keep an up-to-date contact list

Refer to records of previous customer meetings if necessary

MAKING A PRESENTATION

Putting over the message in a face-to-face presentation or in front of a large audience is the leading edge of selling. The difference between an excellent and poor presentation is very often the difference between making and losing a sale.

63 Keep your talk as short as you can, keep to the point, and end positively.

PLANNING YOUR PRESENTATION

Although each sales presentation needs to be tailored to both customer and product, there is a basic sequence that will ensure that the audience's initial interest results in action:

- Explain the unique advantages of your particular product or service;
- Emphasize all the successes that the product has achieved, and back up your claims with up-to-date statistics and endorsements from other customers;
- Explain that it would be dangerous to lag behind in the marketplace;
- Aim to persuade the audience that the purchase of your product or service will improve their status in the market;
- Finally, encourage the audience to act immediately to guarantee fulfilment of their order.

TIMING THE TALK

The rules of a presentation are the same as those for a good speech. First of all, set down the key points you wish to make in the AIDCA sequence (see pp. 34–7). The shorter the time taken to present them the better: 20–40 minutes is the typical attention span of most people. Divide the number of points into the allotted time, and you then know how long to spend on each point. If using visual aids, as you should if possible, three minutes is probably needed to make each point. This means that you can make only ten to twelve points in all, but this is usually sufficient.

▼ **USING EMPHASIS**
Reinforce the main points of your presentation by first giving the audience an introduction to your speech, then discussing the issues you raise, and by finishing off with a clear summary.

| Tell them what you are going to say | Say it | Tell them what you have said |

▲ AUDIOVISUALS
High-level technical AV aids may require specialized help to set up. Always have a technical rehearsal before the presentation.

USING AUDIO-VISUAL AIDS

The mind remembers speech less well than images, and images alone are registered less efficiently than an audiovisual (AV) combination. Using top-quality AV is far easier than ever before – thanks to personal computers and the software that creates colored texts, images to order, and animations, and projects them digitally onscreen. For face-to-face meetings, a standard computer screen is fine. But to create maximum impact, you should go for a full-color projection, with dynamic, moving elements, a soundtrack, and perhaps lighting effects. Always tailor the AV presentation to the perceived needs of the customer.

ACHIEVING IMPACT

Effective messages are easy to recall, convincing and distinctive, and are stimuli to action:
- Be emphatic about the benefit you offer, and start with an arresting statement;
- Follow the golden sales rule of addressing solutions not problems, and introduce your product or service (visually and aurally) at the earliest possible moment;
- Repeat the company or brand name frequently.
- Never knock the competition: explain that your excellent offer improves on their good solution;
- Do not overemphasize technology, which can lose a nontechnical audience;
- Sincerely mean what you say, and say only what you mean;
- Finally, end with a repeat image of the product or service and the company.

64 Develop a new set of audio-visual images for each new talk you give.

65 Do not read your speech – memorize as much as possible.

NEGOTIATING THE TERMS

Even when the customer has agreed to give you business, you still have to negotiate terms and conditions. Any two negotiating sides will probably have different objectives. Be prepared for these differences, and work toward mutual satisfaction.

66 Analyze what you would do if you were in the other party's shoes.

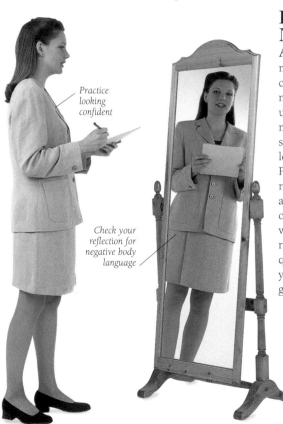

Practice looking confident

Check your reflection for negative body language

PREPARING TO NEGOTIATE

Anticipating what the buyer may say or ask gives you a critical advantage at the negotiating encounter. If you are unprepared, a single question may ground your whole strategy. Poor preparation has lost many sales contracts. Prepare to your best ability by rehearsing with colleagues, asking them to assume the role of the customer. Concentrate on what questions are likely to be raised, how best to answer the questions, and how, through your use of body language, to gain the customer's confidence.

◄ TRIAL RUN
Practice what you will say to customers before a negotiation, preferably in front of a mirror so that you can check your expression and body language and keep both positive. You will then feel better prepared and less anxious about the possible outcome of the meeting.

46

MEETING THE NEEDS OF BOTH PARTIES

Your goal is to make a sale on terms that satisfy the needs of your business. That goal should always include meeting the needs of the buyer. Come into the negotiation, therefore, with a clear idea of your own and your company's best, medium, and lowest acceptable outcomes. You require an equally clear idea of the customer's expectations. The first task in the negotiation is to confirm that your analysis of your own and your company's needs is correct. If not, adjust it accordingly. Next, be seen to work toward the customer's needs as far as possible.

▼ COMBINING OBJECTIVES
Clearly explain your objectives to the customer, and listen carefully to theirs, then work toward combining both sets of objectives for a successful sale.

Customer confirms her requirements

Salesperson explains his objectives

---

67 Avoid thinking in an adversarial, pugnacious style – keep your tone sympathetic.

STRESSING BENEFITS

The purchaser will never mind beating you down to an unprofitable figure. You can try to escape this trap by emphasizing valuable features. However, it is far more effective to stress benefits in terms of time, efficiency, and competitive advantage to the customer. The absolute price is less important (provided it is within the customer's means) than the perceived value for money.

COPING WITH THE COMPETITION

In any negotiation there is usually an invisible third party: your competitor or competitors. Their existing offers have set a ceiling on what deal you may make. The customer will pay more than the lowest competitive offer (or accept less than the best terms) only if you provide a convincing argument for your superiority. Find out all you can about the competition and tackle it head-on.

68 Never criticize the competition, but always aim to outperform it.

SETTING THE PRICE

Effective selling means avoiding price reductions for two reasons. First, price is often not the customer's major preoccupation or need. Second, price holds the key to your profit. Offering price reductions as your chief negotiating ploy may threaten a company's financial returns without making the sale more certain. You will do better to negotiate the price upward. Car dealers, for example, achieve this by offering desirable extras. Given the chance, however, salespeople will generally discount prices as much as they are allowed. Equally, they will resist price rises for fear of damaging volume. The mathematics show that it is much harder to gain profits by cutting prices than by raising them. So, give way on price reluctantly and as little as possible.

POINTS TO REMEMBER

- The most effective negotiating tactic is to stress benefits.
- Emphasizing valuable features is always worthwhile.
- Improving the customer's knowledge of your product or service is a major key to a successful outcome.

69 Initially, ask for the highest price that the market will bear.

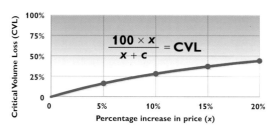

$$\frac{100 \times x}{x + c} = CVL$$

Critical Volume Loss (CVL): 100%, 75%, 50%, 25%, 0
Percentage increase in price (x): 0, 5%, 10%, 15%, 20%

KEY **x** = Percentage increase in price   **c** = Price minus
     y = Percentage decrease in price   direct costs (%)

◀ RAISING PRICES

*This equation helps you decide if you can set a higher price by showing how far sales can fall before profitability declines. In this example, where **c** equals 25, if the product price is raised by 20 percent, profits will not fall until sales drop by more than 44 percent (Critical Volume Loss), making this a risk worth taking.*

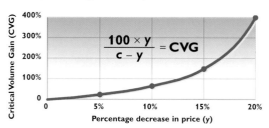

$$\frac{100 \times y}{c - y} = CVG$$

Critical Volume Gain (CVG): 400%, 300%, 200%, 100%, 0
Percentage decrease in price (y): 0, 5%, 10%, 15%, 20%

◀ LOWERING PRICES

*This equation helps you decide if you can cut your product prices by showing how far sales must rise at the new price in order to sustain profits. If the product price is dropped by 20 percent when **c** equals 25, sales must rise by 400 percent (Critical Volume Gain) to maintain profit levels. This is clearly not a viable strategy.*

USING HIGHER AUTHORITY

If you reach an impasse on price, try making a concession that will leave the buyer feeling victorious. Turn to higher authority to achieve this, or encourage your team to turn to you. This backup is needed to maximize the appearance of flexibility, and also for support when standing firm. One Dickensian character used to deal with clients by reference to a senior partner who, in truth, had taken no part in the firm's affairs for years. Avoid making exceptions, however, that seriously undermine the value of the sale.

70 Try to keep the negotiation on a friendly level at all times.

▼ SEEKING CONSENT
Leave the room to find or call your superior, and come back with a special concession for the buyer: "My boss says he can make an exception in this case."

71 Be ready to refer upward any sales problem that you cannot resolve.

Manager's involvement increases perceived value of concession

Salesperson seeks senior approval for special deal

CLOSING THE DEAL

To close a sale you need to lead the customer to the point at which he or she feels confident in accepting your offer. Provide as much information as possible, resolve any objections, and ask for a decision – but avoid applying pressure.

72 Take note of any considered objections.

CONSIDERING THE CLOSE

To close you need to behave in a way that directly or indirectly prompts the buyer to commit to the sale. Avoid acting according to a predetermined formula at this stage – you are dealing with an individual and should plan your closing with that in mind. Some customers like a direct approach; others find this hostile and prefer a choice of options, or some last-minute reassurance.

Customer likes benefits and accepts terms

Salesperson deals with objections by stressing the benefits of the sale

▲ REACHING A CONCLUSION
Avoid set rules to close a sale. Instead, stress benefits and, if necessary, use a final concession to secure your sale.

73 Thank your customer warmly, whatever the outcome has been.

OBTAINING FEEDBACK

Customer objections can be discouraging, but high objectors are nearly three times as likely to buy than prospective customers who offer no objections at all. Non-objectors give the salesperson low feedback of any kind and make the selling task harder. In contrast, the objector is reacting, entering into a dialogue, and giving the salesperson a cue for the next move. Never lightly dismiss objections from customers, but take them as serious matters for discussion toward the closing stages of a negotiation.

GUIDING THE CUSTOMER

Wait until you feel that you have given and received as much relevant information as possible to enable you to guide the negotiation to a successful conclusion and generate a decision to buy. Then summarize all the key points made, emphasizing the strong links between the customer's objectives and your product or service. Ask the customer if all concerns have been satisfied, as this helps to clarify the situation and gives you a final opportunity to defuse any lingering resistance.

FINALIZING THE SALE

It is important to act swiftly and not to allow the buying moment to pass. When the time has come to sign the contract, the customer will clearly see that the benefits you are offering correspond exactly with their needs, and the buying decision should be a mere formality. Have your pen and the order form on the table during the negotiation to avoid introducing them suddenly, which may give the impression that you are pushing the customer into the purchase.

74 Identify success criteria beforehand, and always work toward them.

75 Analyze your successes as closely as your failures, and repeat techniques that lead to success.

76 Look for lessons when you fail, and learn from them.

PHRASING YOUR CLOSING QUESTIONS

Asking the buyer for a decision can be awkward, so find some closing phrases that you feel comfortable with. Aim to introduce the close as a natural progression of the negotiation by asking questions that assume a positive decision has already been made:

❝ What delivery date would be most convenient for you? ❞

❝ Do you have an order number or any other order references that I need? ❞

❝ Should we send the invoice to the delivery address, or would you prefer it to go to head office? ❞

❝ Of course it's cheaper to order in bulk, but would you prefer a smaller batch to begin with? ❞

MANAGING SALES TEAMS

Short-term sales management involves daily administration, while long-term management requires decisions affecting the future of the team. Aim to acquire skills for both needs.

LEADING A TEAM

The key to effective sales management is to keep control while motivating salespeople to maximize their contribution as members of a strong team, including key people from different departments.

 77 Give rewards for team success if you want better team performance.

THE NINE SKILLS

Better managers will result from training that covers these skills:
- Recruiting salespeople
- Training salespeople
- Coaching salespeople
- Allocating customers
- Monitoring call rates
- Monitoring performance
- Analyzing sales results
- Rewarding achievement
- Dealing with failure

ACQUIRING SKILLS

The sales manager has a challenging role. You are responsible for hitting sales targets, but you probably do no selling yourself. You may be a promoted salesperson with no experience of, and perhaps little aptitude for, management. This is a common problem. If it applies to you, try to secure yourself some training, and make sure that members of your sales team are provided with training before promotion to management. In your role as manager, always avoid reverting to the role of salesperson, and watch out for this tendency in other members of your team.

RETAINING PEOPLE

The keys to running a successful sales team are providing motivation and recognizing success. Be aware of levels of satisfaction among your team. The best salespeople differ from the worst in their reasons for leaving a company. The champion sellers are most demotivated by bureaucratic restraints on their activity. The low performers put reward first and restraints bother them least. Having unnecessary controls is a poor reason for losing your best sellers.

TOP REASONS WHY STAFF LEAVE

TOP PERFORMERS	POOR PERFORMERS
1 Excessive restrictions	**1** Inadequate rewards
2 Dissatisfaction with job	**2** Lack of prospects
3 Lack of prospects	**3** Dissatisfaction with job
4 Inadequate rewards	**4** Relations at work
5 Relations at work	**5** Excessive restrictions

▼ PROMOTING A TEAM APPROACH
Encourage all departments to exchange information constantly. This will improve each departments' understanding of the business as a whole and create a more competitive workforce.

HARMONIZING TEAMS

Your sales teams should work closely with marketing, customer services, and product manufacturing departments. Ensure a flow of information between departments at all times. This will instantly create a competitive advantage. High-level selling, for example, may be hogged by the marketing staff, but this kind of clannish departmental thinking is as counterproductive as having too many people calling on the same customer.

SALES   MARKETING

MANUFACTURING   CUSTOMER SERVICES

TRAINING YOUR TEAM

Make use of the fact that training works more effectively in sales than most other areas of business. Listen to and learn from the best experts, engage them to speak directly to your team if possible, and allocate sufficient time to training needs.

78 Take notes of what the experts teach, and refer to the notes regularly.

QUESTIONS TO ASK YOURSELF

Q Does the team need to know more about the company's products and services?

Q Do they have a high enough level of technical knowledge?

Q Does the team need to know more about the marketplace?

Q Would performance improve with general sales training?

Q Should training be in-house or out-of-house?

BROADENING KNOWLEDGE

Salespeople are, unfortunately, often treated as technicians who require only sales techniques and product knowledge. Send your salespeople on courses on general business principles and practices to help both them and the customer. The salesperson will better understand the customer's financial needs, for example, and the needs of his or her own company. Such training will also enable the development of more effective lists of high-probability potential customers. Basic knowledge of marketing, additionally, will align the salespeople's message to that of the company's promotional activities.

CASE STUDY

John was the team's new sales manager in a company whose practice it was to fire each month's bottom performer. When that happened to Alan, he complained to John that even Jane, the top performer, would do no better in his difficult territory. The sales manager realized that Alan would benefit from on-the-job training and coaching. John sent Jane to the area and she accompanied Alan on the calls, observed his mistakes, told him how to correct the errors, and continued to train him until Alan eventually topped the team. As sales manager, John responded by pairing all the underperformers with top performers to achieve similar results. The aces were trained in teaching, and the incentives were altered to reward team success as well as individual performance. John's team rapidly improved until it out-performed all other teams.

◀ **TRAINING IN TEAMS**
The sales manager in this case could have easily continued with the crude system the firm used to motivate sales teams. Instead, he listened to an objection, and found a superior system built on training and coaching within teams.

79 Try to engage the experts you respect most.

▼ FORMAL TRAINING
An expert trainer covers a wide range of topics according to the needs of the group. Ideally, the trainer will also be an experienced sales manager.

USING THE EXPERTS

The extent of expertise available in sales training is greater than in any other field of management, partly because so much training is carried out, and partly because it is eminently practical. Professional expertise can be acquired either in person or in recorded form for the reinforcement and expansion of internal training. It may seem costly, but it will pay for itself in improved company-wide performance. Learn how to train other people yourself, as sales managers should be excellent trainers as well.

Salespeople pick up training skills as they learn

Expert entertains with vivid rules of thumb and advice

80 Teach all salespeople business finance principles, no matter how unfamiliar they may be with money matters.

81 Keep your team's technical knowledge right up to date.

USING ROLE PLAYING

The chief value of role playing, with the participants alternating in the roles of buyer and seller, is to train people to recognize and handle a variety of reactions. Different kinds of buyer will react differently: some types will always be eager to buy; others will be almost impossible to sell to. A key issue is how realistic you or your team members are about what your performances can achieve. Buyers can be divided into easily recognizable types (aggressive or suspicious, for example). Acting out how to handle each of the types ensures that selling opportunities are not misread and that time is not wasted.

82 List those who require coaching, and provide suitable training.

83 Make role-playing as realistic as you can for maximum effectiveness.

Salesperson

Hostile customer

Interested customer

Salesperson

▲ **REVERSING ROLES**
Acting out different selling scenarios is an enjoyable method of training. Encourage people to explore a variety of customer responses by reversing the roles each person plays.

ACTING AS COACH

You cannot teach sales skills solely in the classroom. The coach, or mentor, has to accompany the salesperson into the field, taking care to leave the sale to the person being coached. It should go without saying that a manager's coaching skills are just as important as his or her other sales skills. Enhanced coaching abilities will actually improve these other skills. The well-versed coach knows how to concentrate on one skill at a time, and does not use team coaching as a substitute for individual mentoring.

84 Let the sales-person take the glory. It brushes off on you.

▼ **MONITORING PROGRESS**
Constantly monitor performance after training. Give regular feedback to staff to avoid the development of bad habits.

POINTS TO REMEMBER

● Constructive demonstrations of different selling scenarios can be made a part of training.

● The temptation to interfere in a training sale must be resisted.

● The defects of trainees should not be harshly criticized.

● Good progress should be observed and faults noted.

● Anything that has been done well should always be praised.

Salesperson learns from constructive advice

Manager gives feedback

USING ▶ COACHING
As this example shows, it is worth making coaching an integral part of working in a team, allocating regular time to it. Combined with an organized approach to planning the working day, coaching can improve the skills and productivity of the whole team.

CASE STUDY
George took over a sales operation that was seriously under-performing, even though the salespeople were well-trained and enthusiastic. He analyzed the sales records and discovered that the morning hours were the most productive for sales, but were used for daily meetings. He also found that one major distinction of the top sellers lay in their use of the telephone to find new customers ("cold calling"). All training and sales meetings were moved to the afternoons and mornings were used for work with coaches. George paired high-achievers and low performers to coach the latter in the best methods, stopping them, for instance, from apologizing for taking somebody's time; the product was valuable "so he should be thanking you." The results improved dramatically.

MANAGING SALES CALLS

T he times of the day when customers can be telephoned are times for selling. Sales calls must always be put above non-sales activities, such as reporting customer contacts and administration. The calls must be planned and their effectiveness measured.

85 Analyze the success of sales calls continuously.

TARGETING THE CALLS

An increase in sales calls should result in more orders, but you have to target your calls to make them effective. Trying to sell vacuum cleaners to people who already own them, for example, will not sell more of them. With large contracts, a team will make fewer calls because of the greater complexity of the orders. In such cases, pushing for an increase in calls may be asking for failure. Always ask the question "What is the ratio of orders to telephone calls?" to monitor the effectiveness of calls.

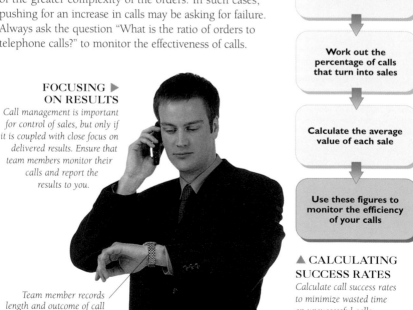

◄ FOCUSING ON RESULTS
Call management is important for control of sales, but only if it is coupled with close focus on delivered results. Ensure that team members monitor their calls and report the results to you.

Add up the number of calls made

Work out the average length of each call

Work out the percentage of calls that turn into sales

Calculate the average value of each sale

Use these figures to monitor the efficiency of your calls

▲ CALCULATING SUCCESS RATES
Calculate call success rates to minimize wasted time on unsuccessful calls.

Team member records length and outcome of call

86 Focus on how many calls result in sales, not on how much time is spent on the calls.

MEASURING TEAM EFFECTIVENESS

The ratio of orders to calls will vary widely within most sales teams. The worst performer may need to make three times more calls than the best. You will also find discrepancies between teams and departments. Such findings enable you to improve the performance of the least effective until their allocated time is used better. You should be able to raise the average ratio substantially by transferring the successful habits and methods of top performers to those of underperformers. Achieve this by allowing less successful callers to sit with top performers while calls are made.

SOLVING PROBLEMS

Both managers and salespeople must manage their call times effectively. Activities that seem highly commendable, such as troubleshooting, may divert managers from their prime duty of maximizing overall customer calling performance. A problem sale may benefit from intervention, but if a manager dashes to every trouble spot, time will be swallowed up or wasted. Treat each difficulty on its merits. Only handle particularly problematic issues, and always consider whether the salesperson – perhaps with some advice – can handle it alone. If so, the experience gained will benefit both the company and the individual.

87 Use your most successful callers to coach weak performers.

88 Resist the urge to interfere or take over every time problems appear.

89 Assume that salespeople can handle problems with minimal help from you.

DO'S AND DON'TS

✔ Do watch closely the call-order ratio.

✔ Do analyze the results of top performers.

✔ Do allow enough time for essential non-sales activities.

✘ Don't push for more calls without a clear objective.

✘ Don't treat under-performers as no good.

✘ Don't feel you have to solve all problems.

PROVIDING REWARDS AND FIXING TARGETS

You may pay your sales team a basic salary, or offer commission or bonuses tied to sales targets. Linking the right payment or incentive to the right target is difficult, but your careful consideration of the link is crucial to your staff's motivation.

90 Keep payments and incentive systems simple and transparent.

91 Make targets ambitious, but keep them within reasonable reach.

BALANCING PAYMENTS

The usual form of payment based on results (PBR) is individual commission, although some companies reward salespeople with salary alone. It is impossible to say which method works best because each has disadvantages. Salary-only provides no reward for exceptional effort, but 100 percent commission provides no security and great fluctuations in earnings. The best schemes combine elements of basic salary, commission, and group rewards.

Salesperson is rewarded for exceptional effort

Manager pays a basic salary plus special bonus

▼ **GETTING THE RIGHT BALANCE**
Combine basic salaries with commissions and group rewards to provide security with added incentives for outstanding performance.

Provide basic pay to cover normal needs	▶	Add commission for exceptional success	▶	Complete pay with group incentives

▲ ELEMENTS OF PAY
Group incentives provide significant extra income for the salesperson. Individual commission provides sufficient extra funds to retain and encourage top performers. Basic pay covers normal personal needs.

SETTING TARGETS

In most companies, salespeople are subject to PBR and targets to a far greater extent than other employees. How you set targets is important, since it determines when commissions are triggered. Involve salespeople in setting all targets – whether standard targets or "super" targets for extra incentives – to establish a logical payment system. This ensures that all targets are set within the upper ranges of possibility and are related to market realities. If this produces a shortfall against goals, then take other actions to fill the gap. Never confuse targets with budgets. A budget is based on what is most likely to happen, while targets are designed to improve on the budget.

92 Involve your sales team in setting realistic targets.

93 Minimize changes to your target schemes. Targets need revising, but too many changes will confuse and demotivate the salesforce.

REVISING TARGETS

Give exceptional rewards only for exceptional performance. If a promotion campaign has already been paid for by the company, do not pay for it twice in undeserved commissions. Target payments have to be revised to recognize changes, to reflect competitive reward structures, and to refresh motivation. Too many and too frequent changes, however, destabilize the salesforce and divert managers' attention. Above all, keep targets and related incentive elements simple and sensible. Many schemes, for example, have a sliding scale for individual rewards that rises to "super" target levels. This can have damaging consequences. For example, salespeople may be encouraged to give away expensive discounts to clinch the "super" sale target.

RECOGNIZING ACHIEVEMENTS

Ensure that you have effective and accurate measures for monitoring the performance of your team. Watch for early indications of success and failure, and provide a solid basis for rewards and incentives.

94 Keep incentive schemes under constant review.

USING INCENTIVE SCHEMES

95 Put actual profits above volume for effective incentives.

Commissions and bonuses in many companies are supplemented by reward schemes using incentives ranging from Caribbean cruises to sports cars to membership in select "super-sales" clubs. These schemes work well as morale-boosters, but they do not serve as a substitute for proper organization, training, coaching, or daily management of the sales force. Regard and treat the incentives as additions only.

MONITORING SUCCESS

Regular checks on sales performance are essential to success, and as sales manager you are responsible for ensuring that these are carried out effectively. You should be aware constantly of several success factors, including market position and realized profits – not just sales volume. The overall objective of sales activities is to achieve optimum revenue and profit while strengthening the competitive position. Thanks to computers, this objective can be monitored more readily and efficiently than before on a daily basis. Once you have identified any gaps between targets and performance, you can initiate corrective actions.

CHECKING PERFORMANCE

For maximum profits and competitive strength, constantly monitor these success factors:

- Realized prices;
- Gross profit margins;
- Company market share;
- Selling costs as a proportion of company income;
- The number of successful sales made by your team.

AVOIDING UNFAIRNESS

The immediate results of salespeople's efforts are visible and measurable. They can point instantly to their successes, but equally they can be blamed for failures. Some companies automatically fire those who miss their quotas. Others fire the unfortunate who comes bottom of their monthly sales league. Both approaches are counterproductive. The prospect of dismissal is intended to motivate, but in reality it achieves the opposite effect. The policy is seen as unfair, and morale is lowered. You should be interested solely in raising the results of the whole team, partly by helping its weaker members.

96 Treat your sales staff as people who can always perform better.

REWARDING SUCCESS

The stick with which "failures" are penalized is usually combined with the carrot – the offer of monetary rewards. Judge performance by measuring customer satisfaction as well as sales volume. Financial rewards and incentives are effective motivators, but are not the only necessary responses to success. People need to feel that their achievements have been recognized. Tell your team how much you appreciate their efforts, and single out the top performers for special praise.

97 Make a public fuss over those who produce excellent results – both one-offs and multiple sales.

DEALING WITH FAILURE

Successes will be accompanied by some failures, which require equally careful analysis. Remember that failure can stem from three main causes:
- The wrong customers were targeted – businesses who are not in the market for your products;
- The customer was right, but the product or service was wrong;
- The salesperson mismanaged the sale.
Penalizing failure only makes any kind of sense in the third set of circumstances. You still need to know, however, why the selling failed.

QUESTIONS TO ASK YOURSELF

Q Was the failure due to lack of selling skills?

Q Was it due to lack of product knowledge?

Q Could knowledge of the customer be lacking?

Q Were any personal problems to blame?

Q Is the salesperson totally unsuitable for selling?

HOLDING SALES MEETINGS

Meetings, conferences, and seminars are valuable for building team spirit, celebrating success, reporting on progress, developing customer relations, and unveiling new plans. Meetings will be most effective if they allow for feedback from the sales teams.

98 Review the annual conference in detail, and always apply the lessons.

99 Ensure that communications can be two-way.

100 Make the team a reality, not just a word that means little to anybody.

BOOSTING MORALE

The mood of a sales meeting will be affected by the latest sales performances, be they acceptable or poor. Whatever the case, do not make the meetings punitive. Constructive criticism, coupled with an objective analysis of the causes of failures, can motivate salespeople and stimulate the desire to do better. However, the goals of achievement, recognition, and reward are more important. Place emphasis on the future, in particular, to boost morale. Make people feel they are part of a team that, despite inevitable and avoidable disappointments, is a real, long-term winner.

CASE STUDY

Anna, who was in charge of a sales operation in the US, regularly received messages from her UK head office berating her for missing her quarterly sales forecasts. If she lowered her forecasts, the pressure became greater still. Anna called her salespeople to an emergency meeting to seek a solution. The teams decided to try pulling in more business for the following three months. After that time, though, they faced even more pressure. The sales force agreed with Anna that the quarterly emphasis made no sense in an industry with a three-year selling cycle, and it was stopping them from winning new accounts. They all agreed that they should shift the emphasis towards three-year plans, broken down into annual targets. Head office accepted the idea, new business flowed in, and the pressure on Anna subsided.

◀ **THE POWER OF MEETINGS**
Anna had a problem stemming from the company's head office. However, by meeting with her sales staff and encouraging them to work together to solve the problem as a team, Anna was able to develop a local solution that met the needs of head office.

HOLDING ANNUAL CONFERENCES

The internal sales conference is often an annual affair, primarily designed to build morale and motivation by celebration and exhortation, and not by specific development of the sales force.

There may be guest speakers – a management guru or a sports personality – but the focus is mostly on rewards. This approach often wastes the invaluable opportunities presented by having all the salespeople together at the same time. Always have clear business objectives, and plan the event around training needs, reaching targets, and giving people a sense of moving forward as part of a dynamic, successful team.

INVOLVING CUSTOMERS

Persuading customers to attend a sales seminar or conference is an excellent method of building the confidence of the salesforce. Your company has the opportunity to associate itself with an authoritative presentation on an important subject (a telecommunications company hosting a seminar on the use of the Internet is one example). Your salespeople can mingle with their customers. Careful choice of speakers will inevitably encourage customers to consider your products and services as first choices. Too hard a sales message, however, will defeat the purpose. That can be left until after the event when you make the necessary follow-up calls.

▼ **RALLYING THE TEAM**
Selling is a social activity, but the socializing must be wedded to very clear business purposes and planned to enable the realization of those aims.

101 Use your seminar as an opportunity to boost customer confidence in your company.

ASSESSING YOUR SKILLS

Selling is the foundation of success in many areas of management. Your sales skills need to be kept strong and up-to-date by practicing and learning. This questionnaire will test the quality of your present performance as a salesperson and show you where you need to improve. To assess your sales skills, add the scores together and refer to the Analysis. If your answer is "never," mark Option 1; if it is "always," mark Option 4, and so on. Use your answers to identify the areas that need most improvement.

OPTIONS
1 Never
2 Occasionally
3 Frequently
4 Always

1 I make a sales plan before approaching prospective customers.

1   2   3   4

2 I develop sales strategies and check activities against a master plan.

1   2   3   4

3 I make a point of learning new sales skills and techniques.

1   2   3   4

4 I use information technology to help organize myself and aid my selling.

1   2   3   4

5 I keep a record of how I spend my time in order to improve its use.

1   2   3   4

6 I identify the customer's needs so that I can vary my approach accordingly.

1   2   3   4

7 I prepare myself carefully before going into a sales meeting or interview.

1   2   3   4

8 I approach companies knowing exactly who is the right person to contact.

1   2   3   4

9 I use research to build my knowledge of the industry and the customers.

1   2   3   4

10 I keep meetings with customers friendly, brisk, and focused.

1   2   3   4

11 I know and use the best techniques for getting sales results by telephone.

1   2   3   4

12 I take great care with my letter-writing and develop writing skills to aid selling.

1   2   3   4

13 I put myself in the customer's shoes when preparing for negotiations.

1   2   3   4

14 I end sales presentations on a positive note, inviting a definite action.

1   2   3   4

15 I ask for feedback on my presentations so that I can improve my effectiveness.

1   2   3   4

16 I adapt my selling approach to match the way the customer reacts to me.

1   2   3   4

17 I tell the truth, even if the truth is not what I want the customer to hear.

1 2 3 4

18 I search for the key sales point that will persuade customers to buy.

1 2 3 4

19 I endeavor to get the other party to name their price objectives first.

1 2 3 4

20 I stress value for money in negotiations, rather than price alone.

1 2 3 4

21 When I complete a sale, both sides are satisfied with the deal.

1 2 3 4

22 I try to anticipate any objections the customer may present to me.

1 2 3 4

23 I respond quickly to inquiries or complaints from any customer.

1 2 3 4

24 I get feedback to ensure that my customers are very satisfied with the purchase.

1 2 3 4

25 I keep other salespeople free from bureaucratic restrictions.

1 2 3 4

26 I use teaching methods to develop my own skills and improve those of others.

1 2 3 4

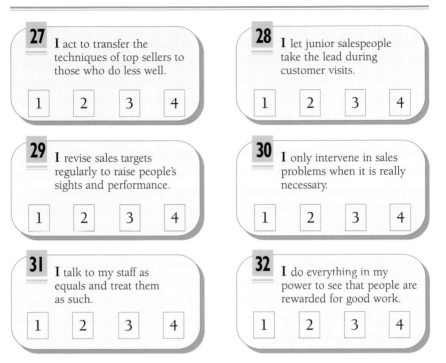

27 I act to transfer the techniques of top sellers to those who do less well.

1 2 3 4

28 I let junior salespeople take the lead during customer visits.

1 2 3 4

29 I revise sales targets regularly to raise people's sights and performance.

1 2 3 4

30 I only intervene in sales problems when it is really necessary.

1 2 3 4

31 I talk to my staff as equals and treat them as such.

1 2 3 4

32 I do everything in my power to see that people are rewarded for good work.

1 2 3 4

ANALYSIS

Now you have completed the self-assessment, add up your total score and check your performance by reading the corresponding evaluation.

32–63: Your lack of sales skills and good practice must be affecting your performance and, possibly, putting your job at risk. Begin at once to master the lessons in this book, and apply them in the office and the field.

64–95: You have made considerable progress and are probably performing well, but you have not raised your sights high enough. Make renewed efforts to improve in the weaker areas revealed by your assessment answers, and continue until your scores take you to the next level.

96–128: You are a skilled and effective salesperson. Continue working to improve your abilities, however, to stay at the top.

INDEX

ACKNOWLEDGMENTS

AUTHOR'S ACKNOWLEDGMENTS

This book owes its existence to the perceptive inspiration of Stephanie Jackson and Nigel Duffield at Dorling Kindersley; and I owe more than I can say to the expertise and enthusiasm of Jane Simmonds and all the editorial and design staff who worked on the project. I am also greatly indebted to the many colleagues, friends, and other management luminaries on whose wisdom and information I have drawn.

PUBLISHER'S ACKNOWLEDGMENTS

Dorling Kindersley would like to thank the following for their help and participation in producing this book:

Editorial Alison Bolus, Michael Downey, Nicola Munro, Jane Simmonds, Sylvia Tombesi-Walton; **Indexer** Hilary Bird.

Design Pauline Clarke, Jamie Hanson, Tish Mills, Nigel Morris, Laura Watson.

DTP assistance Rob Campbell.

Photography Steve Gorton; **Photography assistance** Nici Harper, Andy Komorowski.

Models Jane Cooke, Felicity Crow, Miles Elliot, John Gillard, Ben Glickman, Richard Hill, Cornell John, Chantell Newell, Mutsumi Niwa, Mary Jane Robinson, Kiran Shah, Suki Tan, Peter Taylor, Gilbert Wu.

Makeup Debbie Finlow, Janice Tee.

Suppliers Austin Reed, Bally, Church & Co., Clark Davis & Co. Ltd, Compaq, David Clulow Opticians, Elonex, Escada, Filofax, Gateway 2000, Geiger Brickel, Jones Bootmakers, Moss Bros, Mucci Bags, Staverton. With thanks to Tony Ash at Geiger Brickel (Office Furniture), and Carron Williams at Bally (Shoes).

Picture research Andy Sansom; **Picture library assistance** Sue Hadley, Rachel Hilford, Denise O'Brien, Melanie Simmonds.

PICTURE CREDITS

Key: *a* above, *b* bottom, *c* centre, *l* left, *r* right, *t* top
Powerstock / Zefa 31, 65; **The Stockmarket** Jon Feingersh 45;
Telegraph Colour Library 20; **Tony Stone Images** Stewart Cohen 12, Peter Correz 19.

AUTHOR'S BIOGRAPHY

Robert Heller is a leading authority in the world of management consulting and was the founding editor of Britain's top management magazine, *Management Today*. He is much in demand as a conference speaker in Europe, North and South America, and the Far East. As editorial director of Haymarket Publishing Group, Robert Heller supervised the launch of several highly successful magazines such as *Campaign*, *Computing*, and *Accountancy Age*. His many acclaimed – and worldwide best-selling – books include *The Naked Manager*, *Culture Shock*, *The Age of the Common Millionaire*, *The Way to Win* (with Will Carling), *The Complete Guide to Modern Management*, and *In Search of European Excellence*. Robert Heller has also written a number of earlier books in the Dorling Kindersley *Essential Managers* series.